A Sunny Place
with Adequate Water

A Sunny Place
with Adequate Water

MARY BIDDINGER

Black
Lawrence
Press

Black
Lawrence
Press

www.blacklawrence.com

Executive Editor: Diane Goettel
Cover & Book Design: Amy Freels
Cover Art: *Extra Innings* by Mark Brabant

ISBN: 978-1-62557-908-9

Black Lawrence Press
326 Bigham Street
Pittsburgh, PA 15211

Published 2014 by Black Lawrence Press.
Printed in the United States.

For your twin sister.

CONTENTS

FORTUNES AND MISFORTUNES

Clearly I was getting nowhere.
I wanted to be the next Moll Flanders.

I felt not of myself, as if roads
had shifted a little. But who was feeling

me, then? Pneumonia was like an aunt
who sends you enormous shorts

with the price tag still on,
then watches you toss them into a lake.

I hated my friends and their weddings.
The cold trickle of children

from a neighborhood school turned
into a simulated knife

fight between warring factions.
My distrust of the establishment left

me somewhat prepared.
I was evacuation-prone, redheaded

and formerly adulterous, cultivated
enough to need no costume

but holiday socks and a ghost train
like in the wedding magazines

my friends suddenly began purchasing
while I was attempting sleep

and other things while standing.
Remember when your biggest worry

was where? And now it's how many
leaves will keep you alive.

COIN-OPERATED RATTLE WITHOUT A SNAKE

At my church they only handled dollars and pigeons.
I was starting to run out of revenue, or bills, or royalties.

That coo inside every baby doll manufactured in 1982?
It belonged to me. And not in the way all the soil beneath

my house belonged to me, or the way you still belong
to me, even though I no longer make the sound unless

accidental. There was no recording studio, just an acre
of wax and some dolls made of rubber with carpeting fur

pasted on top. A red brick building. Only one microphone,
but after I stepped up they packed it all away, even

the trailer filled with starlight mints. My church moved
into a trailer after the first fire. After the second fire

we moved instead. Who knew windows were flammable,
that air was only rented? My parents didn't take a penny.

It was somewhat disturbing. By 1986 they counterfeited
my coo in numerous countries, while local high schools

forced teenagers to carry my coo around as a punishment
for displaying hickeys, or licking drinking fountains.

One woman returned her baby to the maternity hospital
because its coo was nothing like mine. Somewhere

a constellation of my voice leaked out of a landfill.
My real body was not nearly as stiff, or as hollow.

AN ELM TREE WILL NEVER BE THE ONE YOU LOVE

As a schoolgirl, all I would do was jump rope
and worry. I tried to make myself into a corner.

I reversed myself until there wasn't anything left.
The worst summer I tied little strings to all

of my edges, secured them onto something
permanent. One tornado after another. One gun

brandished in the Jewel parking lot. I belonged
to no other place than this. When the Dutch

Elm rumors started, our neighbor threw pot
after pot of boiling water on the tree in her yard.

This wasn't a preventative measure. One woman
thumped her trees daily with a rolling pin, or cut

little pieces of bark to hex. My own shards were
not planted in the transom of any public edifice.

I was forbidden to wear paisley, or hear the sound
of a harmonica. It occurred to me that things

were either out, or they were in. Only one man
in the entire allotment had been to Holland.

Nobody spoke to him, or accepted his toy clocks.
They didn't help him roll the fallen barrels back

up his driveway. We held our breath at the sight
of tulips in bloom, hems risen conspicuously high.

AND I WILL NEVER BE THE SAME

Disengaged from the root like a saint
and tumbling our way
on the undulant backbone of a sheet

stripped from somebody's bed, hung
with thumbtacks
from the library cork board. One hoped

they washed the sheet first, cigarette halos
clustered midway
between his dent and hers, the seventies,

any variety of specimens possible, some
even exotic (a love of all
items mango, apricot, fluorescent).

If anything, it made the tumbleweed
look more natural,
in the way I tell you that nobody waxed

where we now wax. It made the weed
look not intruder
or metaphor for the wandering soul

who sidles into town and impregnates
every other mattress
with bedbugs, but like just another organ

in a church like the one we all vomited in
as penitent teenagers.
The hangover invented well before the ax.

Women still smoked in the library, clouds
of Pall Mall creeping
over the great turmoil of the tumbleweed.

I did not wish that I could bring it home
in my underpants,
which was unusual. I wanted to stomp it,

uncoil the filmstrip that brought it there.
Confront the librarian
regarding certain overdue fines levied

against my account in 1979. My father's
horror at the materials
I had allegedly checked out and kept.

At that time I had no inhabitants, summer
dry and humorless.
I had one mother and a room full of other

children, and a sepia box projected upon
a daisy backdrop
until the weed rolled its way out the door.

A COIN-OPERATED PICKAX

I continued standing beneath the same tree
and I admit it. We all kept grinding

our respective pestles into the assigned
mortars, despite the lack of intrinsic beauty.

I willed the ends of my hair into a firecracker.
It was an empty firecracker that only had

light, and no sound. The tree was oblivious.
Nobody ever thought of chopping it,

and what a pity, but it never caused a stir.
I was three years old and standing on a table

in a fish market, kissing old men on the cheek.
My mother told this story every day,

recalled the special on *whatever washed in*.
The man at the counter said it with an accent

and it was so revolting that we purchased
the entire lot. They say guts are the best way

to a less anemic garden. I had what you might
call *the exact opposite of reservations*.

BURYING THE APRON

We didn't have a miniature lighthouse
or a hammer, but thankfully the things we did
have outweighed the things we didn't

such as airplane tickets and apricot jam
(none, and very little) or proper footwear, wet
patches in the yard good for growing

weeds, not people, but that's not to say
we were stunted. Every year my birthday gift
was a trip to the Christmas theme park

that contained a strange number of fires
and other threats to Santa, or the dark house
where they'd put a towel over your

mother's face and pretend to slit
her corduroys with an oversized tree saw.
And then, all that ice, everywhere....

Less than a mile from the park
there was always a girl in her front yard,
hair so transparent it was more like

water haloing her head. Some
kind of radio signal gone solid. Maybe
in a distant dimension

we were sisters. She didn't
seem to have a mother, but if they buried
her apron close enough

to the house, maybe she could
return once in a while, leave spare teeth
in a jar of honey marmalade.

THE SUMMER OF ELECTRONIC MONITORING

All of the boys in town were on tether in the summer of 1987. You'd stroll to the corner store for some Slim Jims, and there they were, pressed against the glass of their attics as you walked by. Sometimes everything was pressed against the glass of their attics, and suddenly the shaved ice looked delicious, or the storekeeper's apron bloomed blood spots at the edges. A few shell casings circled each other on the counter. My mother used to frequent a hair salon filled with various pendulums, or wave-in-a-box machines that sent me running for the bathroom. Those ladies must have been batshit by the end of the day, all that clacking. So what did seventeen-year-old boys do in their attics, the twin beds with bare mattresses, and were those really their rooms, or did they have proper bedrooms downstairs, haunted by air freshener pods? If you asked the boys, they were studying, not tying you to a load-bearing beam of some sort, or running the blade of a knife down their tongues. The walls repositioned themselves like an arthritic cat in a cardboard box. Somebody had left a pile of things from the 1950s up there, and you wanted to be the girl in the homemade dress and white gloves, greeting her date at the front door. His oxford shirt may have been pleated by an exceedingly hot iron, but he had both feet on the lawn. Two flights down from the attic, a hideous grandmother was always boiling a pot of stockings. She never noticed the blood around your mouth as you pushed through the kitchen and out into the garage. She never thought to loan you the best doily in the house.

SOME DISCIPLINE

The punishments were just as lavish as the draperies.
Every other soap dish was really someone's eye
in detention. The chandeliers did not burn oil or wick.

And there I was, cradling my Cornish game hen
two weeks into a sentence of five. Nobody wanted a kiss
as much as a book of matches or sturdy rope.

At first I believed the hen would speak, or at least try.
The roaster left a shine upon its back, a glaze
that reflected the hideous cranium of each brownstone

on the block where I grew up. Black windows
upstairs for the clockmaker, that tiny plastic geranium
never to drop its false squirrels to the sill again.

There was a book about a melee, and how I could not
start one of my own, no matter how passionately
I prayed for it. Like trying to remember a day when

there was no such thing as a lemon, just a chill
expanse of something undisciplined. A pile of wool
at the bottom of the butter churn. So useful

in a way that never made its own sense. I dropped
my hen from the only tower I could open.
The gust of air we felt was no stranger than the sky.

A COIN-OPERATED RAILROAD

In the model train version, you gave me three
breasts, but never touched any of them.

I was making a gesture you described as *tearing*
a retainer from tangles of hair rampaged

both intentionally and not. I missed those cards
that had opposites on opposite sides, so all

the world would know what was farthest from
a sailor with a pink neckerchief, or what

would kill a bulldozer with some true finality.
My tautologies weren't taut at all, so I

did what anyone else would do. I departed
then re-embarked. Doubled my nothing.

Climbed the frost-tip tree that was no tree
but just a daub of glue to seal a root.

A TINY POISON EYE

You see, I had enough of all the rocks.
Of the counting names, and naming hoops
full of air. Like somebody peddling trophies
at a garage sale. Like anyone would fall
for that same sort of thing more than once.
And I do not want to see your magic arm,
even if it's gold. The tea bags constructed
of authentic muslin, presenting themselves
as a miniature sanctuary. I was among
things too small to see with naked eye. I was
among an inhospitable element. Like anyone
would fall for the trick of what's in my
pocket. It's not so much the peddling of
trophies, but buying them. Like my name
was Matilda, and I could fit so much water-
melon in the cannon I built with my father
under a piece of corrugated plastic. My name
was your name and we coalesced until
we were both altar boys, until we cut hands
on the same pricker bushes, dropped our
lunches in the same puddles, vanquished
duplicate enemies. You see, I had enough
to go on, and then I got even more. Magic
arm, no magic arm, my grandfather took his
eye out and everyone screamed. Like anyone
would fall for that same sort of thing more
than once, or more than twice. It's not so
much the eye but the hand that holds it.

COIN-OPERATED ENGINE FINDS
ITS STEAM

The coin-operated Abraham Lincoln had been whacked
in the rear by a tin woodpecker for the last time.

The coin-operated opera singer tried country. Somebody
invented the coin-operated machine gun that night

then realized it would make a better disco ball. Hamsters
were better when coin-operated. Sex was slightly more

inflammatory, but only at first. All these contact allergies,
as if we hadn't already been living in heavy metal.

The Laughing Sal did not run on coins. She ran on fingers
and our own collective agony. The golden goose

did nothing but peck, and would settle for wooden dimes.
The first night we were alone together, I asked

what drove you, and where. Why would a grown man harbor
such an enormous jar of change, if not to sinker

a burlap bag with my body sleeping inside? The first time
I really looked inside your mouth, I noticed a lack

of fillings. So I saturated you. It was the only thing I could
do at the time. Your tattoos were all coin-operated.

The hair under your arms was coin-operated. I operated
on myself until I was right enough to suit you.

We woke a stranger to notarize the name of our operation.
One coin-operated flea sprinted away from its circus.

PICK-YOUR-OWN

Thousands of abandoned fruit stands across
Michigan, but you had to lose
your silver bracelet in mine, or the one I loved

to pretend was mine, its vacancies
so much more tragic than the others, which still
had crêpe-paper birds in rafters.

I thought there would be an endless supply
of choppy water, inferior
rowboats still predictable enough to rock

more than recommended.
Every town with its own hills and houses
like witch teeth. Some day we

would be the people dining in restaurants,
not standing outside them.
We'd give our charity ham to another family.

Buy tickets to something
annual. When the apple pickers finished
we'd reclaim the stands.

You would take the rails apart with an ax
and a little anger. You
always had the jaw for that kind of work.

I was born in the state
that invented its own name, then flooded it
with a hundred miles of lake.

A COIN-OPERATED *HOW DO YOU LIKE ME NOW*

My blood really wasn't that bad, after all. I rocked
the wrong boats, left paper money in fountains

instead of coins. My dog was so beautiful, mistaken
for a more comely sister. I put coats on all the trees

in the nursery, before they fired me. They blamed it
on my imperial attitude. My family was in the vending

dynasty. Our house was made of retired butter knives.
And in every teen magazine circa 1987, the back

of my head, supernova of curls hurricaned by elite
fan placement and a protein made from dried veal.

A network of scaffolding worn close to the scalp.
Not like the shredded ham of a kerchief my neighbor

bolted onto her rollers, but transparent chainmail.
A beehive without the bees or the buzz, invisible

honey. We had a photo shoot in Guam, and kids
snuck their sugar tablets into my collar, bargained

for my Canadian quarters. Nobody ever knew
I was an American, and I did not set them straight.

MINIATURES

They said it was a record
year for being small. Tiny
was the new gray, the new

nudity, only without all that
airbrushing. My man thought
there should be a Y in August.

My man told me don't ever,
but I always did. Who was he
to predict what rained, or how?

My mother called me a complete
disappointment, as if it could be
partial, some kind of equation.

But I could paint the millimeter
stretch of bisque inside the fawn's
ceramic ear. Write my name in

cursive with two eyelashes, still
attached. It was a record year
for bone-crushing. People drank

from teacups smaller than tears
and wrestled on linen napkins
spread out on threadbare lawns.

The new competition of who
could defoliate the fastest, elms
and birches slapping down all

day long. After a while nobody
even cared to fetch the chainsaw.
My mother told me to diminish

myself using any available means.
I told her to cast herself in clay.
The kind you crush in your hand.

A COIN-OPERATED ARBORETUM

It was the year the trees decided
to kill each other, and then us,

and then each other again.
Finally the horizon was an eye,

which was better than a hook.
The sweet hole you kept digging.

I wanted to be your best meadow.
It was hard to appear natural

when certain angles couldn't
exist on their own organically.

Such as this one, here. The point
was that we rode an entire year

like it was a bull, or an escalator.
A hundred houses on a hill, but

damn my decimals. We'd be inside
none of them, and they would never

be inside of us. Only a few select
days could be defined as temperate.

Nobody digs holes in the weather.
A widow lived behind me as a child.

She covered her mouth every time
she spoke across the fence. I must

have learned it from her, the way
I hide my face when not required.

My mother accused all my friends
of being deceptive. She was right

on one count. I would become
something she did not make me.

FIGHT OR FLIGHT

I am uncomfortable discussing my assets
in a room filled with artificial lambswool
and all our first husbands or wives.

At least it looks that way. I'm original
because I still exhibit the Moro reflex well
into my twenties. You should see me

when the bus backfires, or a shirt on a bed
turns into a wild hog. These goods
are self-damaged. I'm addicted to knives

of light across the highway, in a place
I shouldn't be, creak of a security guard
belt in the hallway. We sleep on books.

We swear too much and sometimes eat
meals then hop off the balcony.
We set a terrible example for your

student teacher, who burns her skirt
in front of the class reading Kant.
That is why I have poignant interviews

with the Quaker college, university
in a state nobody has visited. I wear your
gold cross. You have written every

word of my cover letter. I am indeed
an adventuress. If I were a death
I would involve lanterns and wet fields.

A SUNNY PLACE WITH ADEQUATE WATER

More magnolias than you could ever count
or would ever want to. We restrained ourselves
as the bee entered one, only to be armied

by ants under every petal. Sometimes
intervention is plain wrong. I wore no emblem
on my clothing. You wore your leather

work gloves until they were as real
as a stillborn calf, and only half as truthful.
There should've been a law against

us marooned in an abandoned brewery.
The irony of it. All of those vats, and empty
aprons. I wouldn't even wear one

for sport. You made me into the best
lieutenant. I had a knack for it, my size, or else
the way I never remembered the right

formula at the correct time. You thought
we should be killing something by now, if only
a mannequin leaning into a cardboard box

on the loading dock. I always had a soft
spot on my skull, like it never fully closed, so
I hated that dummy all the more. Might

we plant her like the bones of a lost
ape, or seat her in the stadium after all fans
had exited the gates? I would not let

you touch her. That was my designation.
I had the gloves for it. Out of her spindles shot
magnolias. There would be no resurrection.

PARLOR GAMES ARE FOR THE WEAK

Calligraphy was for girls with nobody
to knife like a tree. Bowling

was for lives that never got lucky.
By the time I had my first

apartment, I kept a lipstick in every
room. There were exactly

three rooms. The garbage chute
backed up seven floors.

Old ladies of ghost vaudeville paid
for pints of gin with dimes

downstairs. Card games, violent
hairpieces, an illegal gray

monkey dressed as a rooster clown.
Certain days I swore they

boiled unpaired boots in the atrium.
Some tenants were never

seen, had Polish maids with elbows
like witch-handles, laundry

hampers and harp buckets. I failed
to comprehend a word.

When I moved out I left the dishes
dirty. Shoved my boxes

across lobby parquet like erasing
half of a one-way trip.

There was no room for degenerate
tea sets. I found a taxi

deep enough to fit my leg bones,
my ravening pincushions.

A MODEL CATASTROPHE

The toothpick pantheon only had to survive
up twelve stairs and across a narrow man-made
bridge, but apparently that was too much.

I rented an extra oven so the soufflés could be
simultaneous in their rise and crash. Traded
battery lanterns for the new kerosene,

which was something my body used to burn
so long ago I was a different person altogether.
Various rings, a denim jacket, indifference.

I was custom made for bus seats, park benches,
like a sugar cube igloo where the hint of
verisimilitude pink looks more hemorrhage

than dimension. Fondant Balto, diorama
Bastille pieced with Pfeffernüsse bundles,
giblet Roosevelt, gravy stain Oklahoma.

I wanted one of the racks of glasses I used
to stack out of the restaurant washer, steam
never losing its enthusiasm. I could cook my

own dinner and everyone else's dinner
as long as that dinner involved multiple pots
and a race to see which boiled fastest.

I was an acre of handmade turf, remains
of a private snowstorm, the kind that upturns
itself, forgets to look back as it frenzies East.

COIN-OPERATED NEIGHBORHOOD FALLS TO RUIN

After a while the meter maids had nothing left
to mete out. So they cleaned the houses we didn't have.

It only took a few minutes. There was some kind of end
to the street, and it was radiant, the way my mother

tortured the batter on a greased skillet. Just a tiny kill.
We all became our own prey, until nobody cared.

Shouted at our likenesses in rainwater, arm-wrestled
the creeping vinca and almost beat it. The maids

became *made*, as in impenetrable. They sold us
our own belongings before we missed them.

We had nothing but our bolts of felt and our rods.
Somebody's church became firewood, char,

then firewood again when the fire came back.
Our city knew better than to build anything for good.

My flock preferred the brisk anonymity of a drive-by
corn stand. Sometimes I valued far too highly

the circular nature of the roof above. The maids
too short to assemble dwellings such as bungalows.

I lacked a fierce mandible, but compensated.
When moorings tore there was simply nobody else.

REVITALIZATION YIELDS QUESTIONABLE RESULTS

Nothing was available downtown.
We just ate our city bread, played another

game of pin the sin on the sinner.
My dog could barely keep her belly off

the sidewalk, and nobody blamed
numerous cuts of faulty pork snapped

from one counter or another.
Was I being tailgated by my successor,

or was I the successor? Hopeful
street sweepers shoved newspapers into

the alleys, as if some hand
had momentarily released them, not

slept on them, wiped with
them. Once this corridor was determined

a resurrection zone, but that
will never explain the trail of sweaters

or the fence spiked with
empty lipstick tubes: a golden beacon

until you get up close
and realize it's another shaming device.

Only some people high
on the corner weren't walking anywhere.

Half the pigeons participated
in a rumble over spilled coffee grounds

while the slackers eluded
all awareness of nylon boots, or traffic,

or the crotchety gasoline
of a sun far too loose with its flares.

SOME DEAD MAGIC

Every last building we crept into was a cathedral
in some way, eventually. Holy scepter of broken

sink and dead pigeons arranged like merchandise.
You could say they *arrayed themselves*. Starlight,

the black plastic bags only the liquor store gave us.
A full set of kitchen knives under the driver's seat,

tucked in a tidy wooden block. Some days I almost
snuck a baguette in there beside them, or an orange

pepper. Not that we ate. It was up Woodward, down
Woodward, and I wasn't the driver, so I was the car.

The bus shelters all piled with babushkas. I said my
own rosary. My mother had carefully written a house

number on an index card, in case someone found me.
She forgot the phone number. I felt my way home

anyway. There were six of us, or only four; we lost
my sister in a bathroom mobbed with wet graffiti.

Those days something was always wet and hanging
above. Even streetlamps couldn't help themselves.

Where could they possibly lead us? There wasn't
any magic left in the world, only stray newspapers.

A COIN-OPERATED LUNG AND A HALF

Once there was a particular halogen candelabra.
It was the sexiest pile of glass I had ever seen. Please
note that this was well before I met you. And how did
they keep it up there, in the ceiling, while all
the time I was lying below it or hunched on a red couch
with a nebulizer or something similarly humiliating.
Hunched on a red couch watching some footage
of my famous pump fake. Or of the two of us barreling
across an intersection in our fire truck, cut with
an interview about some asshole and his knee surgery,
or some lady being wheeled on a stretcher
and the asshole with the knee asking if she had metal
anywhere special and could he peek. The knee
had nothing to say. It wanted one of those synthetic
coffees from the machine. It wanted a Betadine swab
or two. They told me, honey, these children
will just laugh at you until you shake a cane at them,
but I wasn't lame. You couldn't call me anything
and perhaps I was not completely truthful.
I took my mother's prize shawl and buried it
between the holly and the other holly. There wasn't
a candelabra, I imagined it. I found a lost knee
on a red couch and hid it under the nearest lab coat.
Halogens aren't glass unless you want them to be.

THE FATE OF THE OLD MILL IS STILL UNDECIDED

We were running across a parking lot and we both had guns. The leaves made an admirable attempt at following us. They called us the followers. They put the twine in our hands and told us to make ourselves a keeper. That's what the coaches always called my trademark snap. I was miserable with the little grid for potholders. My potato stamp looked like a raging middle finger. The kind of thing that would never pull the trigger. It was supposed to be a palm tree. Once I ran from one end of a bus to the other. It was a city bus and it smelled like bologna. My teacher made me stand for twenty minutes facing a blank wall. It was the punishment for thinking in palm trees. I heard a song once about running with a gun, and how sometimes the gun was the one running. My mother chained herself to the old mill but she was months too early. The lady two houses away imported a palm tree into her yard, and it was dead before it hit the soil. Somehow all the songs on the radio were about running. My grandfather paced back and forth in the kitchen. There was no *we* back then. You were too busy hovering above the dead, or stealing koi from the municipal pond. My grandfather threw bricks through the busses and they just kept driving. My mother said it was never too early to chain yourself to the one you love.

HAVE MERCY ON ME

Our storage was so cold, and our time
so ordinary, that often we dug holes
in the hillside just to fill them up again.

But that was only a metaphor. The cool
violence of your sweet talk. My red
nightgown abandoned on the highway.

We played the Eucharist game. It was
horrid, but imaginative. Let's say
no strawberries will ever grow in certain

pockets of our house. Like malt liquor
or a denim jacket concealing some.
At first I wasn't even sure you generated

blood pressure, your perfection and all.
Thought you might transcend it.
As a child I spent too much time gazing

at an unsightly portrait on a dry cleaner's
back wall. Somebody painted her
by numbers, but forgot that lips needed

a sliver of white to make them alive.
She became the hideous dolly
of your nightmare. I killed her with things

like gemstones, a rabbit's foot dyed blue,
or the longest knife imaginable
tied to the second longest knife imaginable

and wrapped in some luxurious velvet.
She'd never heard of me before.
She did not hear me coming. I shoot

first, always, and think later. Consider
the first time we saw each other.
I said, Lord, take your hands off me forever.

JEWELRY IS FOR THE WEAK

This world is not for me
but I refuse to shout into a phone

in front of a boarded-up Korean
restaurant. I'm better in bed

with a fever. Sometimes all I have
is a reputation, and that

doesn't watch the children
for long. The books I read did not

prepare me for the unenviable
bottom rung of citizenship, days

scrubbing the neighbor's toilets
announced themselves

as temporary, a quaint scene
in a woodcarving that turns out

to be a subversive beast fable
I explain to students

using an old fashioned pointer,
the chalk-tipped kind.

The nuns trusted me, though
my socks were uneven.

The nuns used old-fashioned
pointers, which now

are probably considered verboten
by the Vatican, phallic,

indicative of simmering
feminism. I wish I could go back

and almost thank them,
but the teakettle is exploding, or

my son has spilled a hot temple
of noodles on the back

of our best dog, since in this
neighborhood you need at least one.

IN WHICH WE SENSE THAT WE ARE NOT ALONE

Various miracles of the most outlandish sort,
and nothing was too heavy to carry.
We had to crouch in the bushes with our nets,

so to speak. Unfurl our maple brown
hair with less caution. They lined me up again,
and the shabbiest bee ever created fell

into a cup of lemonade, almost finished, but not.
The lesson here was supposed to be in
pragmatics. My supporting materials long gone,

left behind the tree where you stripped
pieces of bark for our lunch spoons, then every
centimeter of cotton and microfiber,

faux lace made with care by a robot in Thailand.
Somehow, a hole in my butterfly net.
The scandal! Chaos in the conservatory, or else

just an extra ripple in an experimental
holding pond. Somewhere a bride tumbled off
the bejeweled saddle made for a pony

but stapled onto a sawhorse for safekeeping.
Our love was more like the ultraviolet
lamp my teacher let me demolish after class

when it suddenly ceased being a lamp.
There was absolutely no word for any of this.
When I say it was no longer a lamp

I mean that it became something of a god.
The trees dropped their trash upon us.
We celebrated with our guns, or lack thereof.

IGNORANT PORTRAIT WITH NIGHTSHADE

The bookseller went by some other name
and sold me fingerless mittens. I read your paperless
letters. Every branch in town turned belligerent
and made me feel as if I couldn't spell. Had breathing
and other problems. Even my own country
with its moon-faced ambulances, its inflammatory
fruit pies, always arriving when we least needed
them. The thing about me, it's the grudges.
It is not attractive. Of my countless selling points
I do not list my exactitude, but testimony
from a cream farmer who tried to purchase my left
arm. It was the day you cut me in quarters
to see if I could pass at market. It took more glue
than the world to get it back, and some parts
will never be quite mine again. Of course now
there's fear of the hatchet, spontaneous blockades,
one attempted but swiftly abandoned siege.
As a girl I put my polka dots on a schedule. I beat
none of them. I walked the streets carrying
a starbust of Lucite beads in my chest, or similar.
I had a team of horses that boiled down to a soup.
My unicorn figurines hovered like a masthead
and did more than scare the squirrels away.
Of course, all of this burned down eventually.
I once had a refrigerator that sang to me, and even
though I knew it was dying, I listened to every word.
From its burrow in the magnetic hills, it still tries
to explain exactly when everything went so wrong.

I never learned to pray the right way. I swallowed
when I was supposed to close my hand around a moth.
My yard grew berries that were far too poisonous
to be extinct. I strung them in a chain around your arm.

A COIN-OPERATED APPLE PIE

Because you hated everything. Even the homeless man
who held a sign that read *PREMIUM*. Even the rim of the sun.

The webs between my old dog's toes, though she wasn't
swimming anywhere, I will admit. The phantom lights I saw

every day on my dashboard, and said baby, this thing
won't choke another mile. You hated both the Venus flytrap

and its intentions. They weren't predatory enough, or set
a terrible example for everything else in the yard.

Next the stupid lawnmower would take pity on petunias,
or roll itself into the bed some night, like a scorpion.

You wanted everything to be authentically American,
even the suffering. We played a game where you create pies

on a screen. It was identical to the card catalogue, just
electronic. They made us bake it with the idea of warm hands.

IN THE BACK SEAT OF HISTORY

We lived in Gettysburg like vagrant
prospectors, driven by the scent
of knees and a profound love of dimes

if by dimes you meant knees, and we
were always kneeling before
one altar or another, making sacrifice

as you called it. Your trunk was full
of coffee filters and insoles.
Somebody stole your brother's bike

and that was all the reason needed.
We broke our melon the old
fashioned way, which is to say

not at all. You'd kneecap that bastard.
I knelt in front of you kneading
the last few pages of John Donne's

Holy Sonnets like an exquisite loaf
of historically-derived rye.
When I got to the end I wasn't sure

if breathing was polite, or necessary.
Later I stood in the alley
wearing red tatters of high school.

Our motel was packed with the cry
from a broken television,
the kind that lived between your ribs.

ALL ROADS LEAD TO WATER

Two deer eating from the same flayed bag
of potato chips, and all I could remember

was the way we idled in traffic for hours
behind a boat named *The Merry Window*.

We paraded through our days as if we
meant them, all the while carrying slivers

of titanium between our skin and jackets.
Somewhere in the distance, a grass mound

was really a buried Volkswagen, skulls
planted somewhere less permanent. Perhaps

in the marsh that once ate your left sneaker
whole. One day in an abandoned bandage

factory, I found your inner shepherd. Stray
fingers of cotton batting, the plastic sheets

that ghost branches of trees on the highway
still rolled in bolts, as if they'd never leave

without coaxing. There was only one sink,
a code violation more blatant than skin

you left behind on the last working lamp.
I stared into its bulb, but didn't need it.

To be two halves of one wet cinderblock
holding up the weight of a thousand bales

of wool. To be both field and the last dog
to survey the edges of where it all began.

A COIN-OPERATED NEIGHBOR TO THE NORTH

I am not such a good speaker. Nobody cares
about Canada, but I try not to believe it. Lightning,
and those cheap plastic boxes of rainbow sugar

that people try to win at roadside casinos.
A trip to Paris that ended up being the Paris
of the Midwest, only just a little higher on the map.

There may have been a bag over my head. I couldn't
get the words quite right. You said something
about loosening your load, or that black and white

scarves were required to eat indoors. They'd stone
around the trees so the deer wouldn't get too
forward. And then it was ninety-one pages, not one

spoon in sight. I carried my typewriter under my arm
and collection of handkerchiefs tucked in back.
It was a real fire alarm, even if the devil was fake.

Up there, a KitKat was like a mobile orgasm in red.
I found myself scrambling up a street in leather pants
that weren't mine, or clutching some old woman

on the electric train, hoping to find the right kind
of bodega. Only it wasn't a bodega there.
They called it a *pitch-wallower.* A *mashhopper.*

Told me to get my blind anklet out of their snare
before they had to call my widget. They could all go
to their walnut-crusted hell. Something was blowing

a classic freight train horn, but it was like a ghost
and not a bit more polite than the alternative.
Somebody was forcing me to eat my dinner

with a sore throat. I didn't choose any of it.
My car was either in the impound lot, or stolen.
The hotel room rolled itself over all night long.

OCCUPATION: HAZARD

Some terrible song involving two magnets
and their unreasonable behaviors. It kept me up
all night. You took me on a ride called *The Scrambler*.

Exchange of foreign currency. Arguments over
things like hysteria and interior diplomacy, space
between one twin bed and the next, even though

conjoined by one rust-colored afghan. Certain degrees
of slippage, so they said bring a map anyway. Hike
your trousers up as far as they'll go, to appear local.

You weren't sure what they meant by customs,
tried shaking with your left hand. Not a good guess.
The forms were like eating an endless bowl of tapioca

without the pleasure of it. I should've been born
something round, maybe a ball bearing. A world was not
an uncertain place. All of my tattoos were inches away

from being misspelled. A line in the paper claimed
my photographs *no longer potent*, and then assaulted
a local bakery for mundane flatware, tore the top

off the couple celebrating 67 years of absolute torture.
My shirts were packed with explosive grudges,
their residue. You said I might need to be reinstalled.

You said that I was really no professional, even though
I put my camera both first and second. Once poked
my own pinhole in the alley outside an illegal

Caribbean nightclub on the outskirts of Des Moines.
I slapped a lady outside the charity auction
and my handprint stayed on her face for three weeks.

There was nothing I wouldn't do to restore order.
I was the maid in the apron handing you a paper towel,
water counterclockwise down every drain at once.

A COIN-OPERATED DIARY

Tuesday, and the anesthesia has all but worn off.
My plumage still intact. My inner workings still

working, or at least issuing an appropriate whir.
Nobody had painted anything on the Dumpster.

I once had the idea to design a dress from curtains
but couldn't tolerate the geometric catastrophe.

And now I am home, making money. Shoplifting
my own belongings, then returning them to myself.

They dispense an elixir for that, and it's thick,
grape or mojito. I invented it, then sold the patent.

Even the most deceptive faux leather can't breathe
with a person inside. I am appropriately terrified

of my god. He can't ever leave me. I attempt to
explain this to every passerby who contemplates

lifting the lid of the Dumpster. Don't do it, brother.
There's a riding mower that never gets close enough.

Any fringe is pure effrontery. It will split the temple.
Crush the steel barrel filled with partial disclosures.

My god would never consider a faux leather mantle,
or conceal all of his business beneath a copper lock.

SWEETS BEHIND THE COUNTER

The woman who sold antique tea cakes
claimed she was selling other people's
disasters, but mostly it was the smell
of cardamom and long-dead panic. Who
would be crazy enough to preserve cake
like a rare stamp or a particularly bold
caterpillar? The entire town was antique,
hard for me to purchase you a real beer
or myself some replacement pantyhose.
They answered sarsaparilla, or woolies,
rent a room upstairs a fortnight, horses
kept and watered extra. And somehow
I was more like the very modern street-
light someone tried to disguise with nets,
dead moths. Who were these people
gathered around a radio, beating it with
a hand-whittled cane, like a box snake?

I once knew a boy from this town, sold
him a round container of facial astringent
for his acne. He paid me in dimes, not
antique nickels. My mother used to make
me walk the arcades with her, translate
all of the objectionable cards into plain-
speak. It was difficult to turn off lamps
because there weren't any in most rooms.
We believed all of the dead objects knew
they'd outstayed their welcome. I had

an impossible time finding reception.
We kept waiting for them to sew us
into our coverlet. The night felt so old
that we didn't bother to close our eyes.

INERT, OR SOMETHING CLOSE

He who did not know the train
from its whistle, who thought my body
was hostile, if not a country in itself

ready for storming. Who held two
sides of the earth apart, then together,
because why not, they matched.

Two buildings faced each other
but weren't reflections. No water
to the top floors, and no steam, ever.

That wasn't where we lived.
Our rooms were full of sunburn
and the way you have to calculate

every inch of the body when under
the suggestion of a siege. This is
to say come on and open your eyes

already. At some point, what you do
becomes something you don't want
to do. But don't ask me. None

of that between my west and east.
I'm only recounting things I've read.
My mouth never has to open.

Sometimes the burn is so much more.
Let's live in it, or turn something
into what it really wanted to be.

THEY APPEAL TO MY SENSE OF LOGIC, AND LOSE

If logical appeals were guillotines, then all of the heads in town would be free. I kept seeing my fate in the mangled pendulums of the daylilies. It looked like someone had loved them too fiercely. I swear it wasn't me. Sometimes my friends tied me to a settee (with angora yarn) and attempted an appeal. Now would a baker want to knead your thigh like a pile of phyllo? Would a fisherman daydream about slipping his hook into your cheek? When the executioner comes home from a day with the chair, or the rope, or the squad, or the specially-trained raptor, why would he want something other than a comfortable chair, a pretzel with hot cheese? When he says he wants to count the number of times you blink, he does not mean your disembodied head. He does not mean blink. He does not mean that he'd line the basket with a cloth resembling your favorite apron. He would part with everything except the velvet canopy of your mouth.

BIRTH OF A VESSEL

It took three tries, and even that
was not enough. Inventors

of the triplicate form
in their most lurid fantasies,

every layer a pastel slip
peeled from the homecoming

queen hours after the last
carnation. The brick wall not

the only one laughing.
It wasn't even real champagne.

The wordless trill
of a mimeograph machine

longing to be manhandled
like years ago. They

put the bottle in my hand.
It shook like a quail.

I wanted to build you the wolf
you never had as a boy.

But they wanted statistics.
Reams of paper

fell from their secret moorings
in the drop ceiling.

What else was a mouth for?
Certainly not licensed

to operate in this state.
I once believed hiding out

was to be expected,
and so I walked spare drywall

sheets up a hill, casual,
the death of all known mystery.

Of course they found me.
A switchboard vomited instead

of retaining its possessions.
I pretended the wall

was a boat. Nobody dared to
avoid calamity.

Inside, the lobby quaked
with ecstasy. I was thankful all

of the dogs on the lawn
had been forced into slippers.

Squeezed into jerseys
with the eponymous logo.

I named the boat *subterfuge*
and I blessed it.

A COIN-OPERATED BUTTON-DOWN COLLAR

You had a job in accounting. You had a wide skein
of pink broadcloth, claimed it as an inheritance, but
who on earth would tax it, as every bee on earth died
for sins committed without the slightest flower. Your
mother held up the convenience store on my street.
She used you as the getaway driver. Nobody shoveled
that neighborhood out. Too bad you hadn't been born.
Of course she really didn't steal anything. There was
no section for sewing notions. Our mothers wanted
nothing but the entire royal wedding. The drinks they
invented while they neglected us. I worked myself all
the way through the storm sewer, only missed when
I wasn't there to fetch more grenadine. You used
the word *math* like it was a sexual innuendo. Some
tailor closed down shop with exactly zero dollars.

BUSINESS POEM

This day keeps getting more and more disheveled.
Someone is having a party in the bathroom.

There's nothing to look at beyond conventional
streamers. I find myself between sizes,

like a semi-abandoned miniature golf course.
I would like to invent an indoor fire pit

for offices that need more violent recourse
than rickrack of sensitive documents.

Once I was like a confidential file. I hid certain
parts with correcting tape. Keyboarding,

they promised, would be the only class we'd use
in our future of damp napkin removal

or ass-slathering. How many just like me turned
not to tricks but massive typing pools

where rewards were Tylenol caps and hot water
to soak extremities. One gal's sweater

was the envy of all the others. Someone calls
my phone looking for a Rebecca.

Our office manager has found an innovative use
for all the defective paper clips.

Dear God, please stop photographing food,
I begged of the mystery caller, who

must have had water running in the background,
or property on the best side of a stream.

VERSION OF MYSELF IN THE RUINS

We filled a paper balloon with corn syrup
then kerosene. The entryway smelled of shoes

and acquaintances. Somebody shoved her
hands into a damp burlap sack of barley.

Wind like a spigot at the edge of the yard.
Such weather made me violently wistful.

I looked like a widow, or an owl handler.
The birdseed bell had no clapper,

neither deer-proof nor silent. I left both
shoes at the party, armed my way down

a path of dead tracks. Rugged as molasses.
Friendly as a mineral lick. For hours

working elbows through mosquitoes
and those vibrating shadows that bicker

under city elms. I was awful violin music,
phone half swallowed by a phantom carp.

You found me between a box of wires
and a shrub the size of a claw-foot bathtub.

I believed the tracks were a harmonica
we could never hear above ground.

A COIN-OPERATED GENTRIFICATION ZONE OF THE HEART

I could never find enough quarters. Even when I worked exclusively for them, as a gypsy in a box. Even when they were the only thing I could keep down. There was a violence in the heather. My city died because we made it die, and then we loved it even more. Suddenly we were authentic, and the stores started carrying our likenesses. But nobody really liked us. They just wanted a piece, so to speak. Once saw a man in a top hat and your old velour sweatshirt I burned while you were drunk under the front porch. We were on a bus, so the man just strolled on by with his pet hangover. It tugged him by a chain. In the photography studio they made you hold me down behind a curtain. You whispered *catastrophe, catastrophe*, like that would somehow get me going. I promise that there was an old neighborhood. It was real, and it was full of wives. They bought that pink dish detergent because it was cheapest. Ironic how later the alderman used it against them, like napalm. They didn't even try to hose me out. I was blocks away, watering some dead begonias. Waiting on a bus for something called an oral history. You told me I'd know it when I heard it. Our place too submissive for a skyline. And all the time we should have been taking notes, while a man and a woman on a bench took notes about us. The police only wanted to know our favorite songs and haunts.

SOME DEAD INGENUITY

There wasn't any room for my inventions.
Even the ones that didn't consume their own
workings within seconds, the way I did.

Some kind of electronic transmission
and sirens went off, but not with enthusiasm.
Flowers near the window well fancied

themselves lovelier than I, and were correct.
The truth was I'd let it all go. Thrilling
how much time is left when nobody bakes

new bread for the new day. The children
preferred to lick postage stamps
anyway, though they were no longer issued

in America. The man next door made
a newspaper flag for his window and covered
the petunias with tinfoil, for later.

Of course it didn't work. Local gangs
used the foil to sell baklava squares or heirloom
tomatoes to anyone half interested,

the way gangs always do. One time I tangled
up with them, the flow of the train car
just paired us together, even in the absence

of my own raging bandana. Like the first
job I had, when the lady told me
there was a tiny fan inside the computer,

bundled in a dust of its own. I must
have been so tender then, because I trembled
for hours and did not recognize

my left hand from my right, violated
what seemed like ten miles of dot matrix paper.
So much like the executioner, who

does not need to show his face, only walks
from the curb with a bag in hand.
The grass keeps swaying until it's all done.

ELEGY WITH FLICKERING LIGHTS

Something like *arrested for solicitation*,
like the underbelly of a boat that nobody saw

for what it was. We pretended an escape hatch.
Our yard had so many chickens it was ridiculous

and so were we. Somehow the marbles became
a commodity worth more than glass. We wore

old-fashioned sleeves and dirty knee socks.
She drew all over her mattress with red marker.

In ten years we'd both have the right touch
for something. It was inevitable. Our dresses

would haunt one man's closet, and then another.
I was always the one mouthing off, getting into

whatever car opened its door. Windows issuing
cologne that smelled like cherry disinfectant.

Halfway through the night we'd swap wigs
and how that would shake everything up.

Once we watched a car fly off the overpass
and crash onto a highway. All I remember was

how the horn blared all the way down. Lights
in the gas station flickered for the shortest

second on record. Then the cash register rang.
A door closed, and I never saw my sister again.

A FRIENDLY STAY OF EXECUTION

Say it was a miscommunication. The sentence was dispensed across the universe at the exact moment a man left his favorite collapsible water glass in the bathroom and had to walk the line between aspirating and not aspirating a lozenge. After all, the executioner only shows up, or doesn't. And when he doesn't, it can be that all is forgotten, somebody's parrot got loose in the documents, and next thing the rapists are baking scones and the burglars are elbow-high in somebody else's corn. The limp-haired pen pal hears a knock at the door. The housewife who learned how to stretch her image thinner using conventional photo editing software drops a jar of pickles and flees. A reformed hustler now reveals to what degree he is not named Lorraine. And I just continue to peel my potatoes, because I am useful. I never run out of things to peel. When the executioner does wake from his stupor, or removes himself from the giant glue trap, he won't pull into the driveway, but I still launch the stigmata. There's a piece of asbestos tape that nobody dares peel away, and no one has the patience to soak until inert. It looks almost whimsical, hanging there, like it could belong to the best-tended bungalow. The executioner's bag has a rip in the bottom, and it is just for me.

A COIN-OPERATED PARLOR

We were all fools, but we still took turns
acting the fool, or playing the fool. *These sandwiches*
are an insult to my pin curls, or *I will not stand*

for such draperies. There wasn't any ether left
in the world, and nobody had the commitment to seal
our deliberations in Argon gas, like etchings by a famous

designer of undergarments, or the ephemeral
renderings of our own founding fathers, who somehow
managed to spill themselves into someone or

another, or the idea of someone. Or an umbrella
hastily left at a bedside, this being centuries ago, when
manners aren't what they are now, and roofs barely

covered themselves, let alone others. Gentility
wasn't invented overnight. We were simultaneously
adverse to and stimulated by the high quality

of the bathroom fixtures. I fancied myself
the opposite of a petunia. I sketched with charcoal
the likeness of my interlocutor, then set up

my pretentious easel and began to feign painting.
My interlocutor exploded into a thousand crystal
goblets. They were all for my mouth alone.

WE INVENT THE OPPOSITE OF VEGAS, THEN TAKE IT ALL BACK

Nobody would sell us a map of Detroit. They gave me
loaves of bread, the signs off the walls, goats tied out back.

And so the blindfolds, the attempting. Knock me like a Pewabic
tile of the past century, so I'll increase in value shortly

before leveling out to nothing. The way my sister and I
once devastated a coconut because we really wanted to get inside.

This town has none of the dazzle. Even the vacuums spill
just a little instead of really sucking. There's no genuine mafia

on hand when I slide into the machine. Too many people trust
their underpinnings to a metal stranger full of holes.

A COIN-OPERATED CITY OF THE PAST

Eventually the circus lost its power. After all,
your father made it with nothing but scrap
and gutted battery shells. That tiger was no tiger,

and the lady just ten bristles from a toothbrush
he'd saved from your elementary days.
Back before I knew your mouth. Back when

every building they made was gray, on purpose.
An objective analysis of our home terrain
would note the squat vigilance of mine, lack

of real Bolivians in yours, on most days. Hush,
you said, somebody will hear us coming.
All of these creatures in tin face, and not an eye

to give testimony. There was a grasshopper
in the rafters, or a ghost firecracker.
So many times you almost burned this place,

or were those my matches that I planted
between your mattress and sheet,
the strands of my hair that I would drape

across your throat, a friendly knife-slash.
We did not know each other, but had
the same Polish neighbor. If you chose red

she would give me the blue. Once I dove
into the ocean at the exact moment
you stopped your car in a mall parking lot

and examined a girl's purple jacket snagged
across a length of chain link. You made
me, didn't you? And all of this time I've been

standing beside the electric rail line, without
a crossing, surveying the electricity.
Nothing knows how to move without you.

SORRY, BUT SOMETIMES YOU DON'T GET TO CHOOSE

A lazy day, every swan a little less violent, the old ladies less critical, a charming breeze off the artificial pond. The executioner is thinking of sex, not murder. Even the squirrels have declared some sort of awkward moratorium. Nobody gets to wear a mask today. I think perhaps I will shoot two guns instead of one, count all the things that can't be taken away. The executioner throws his magazine in the trash, but it seems lighthearted. Years ago I was backing out of the room where my ancient dog occupied her iconic green sofa. It should've been raining chrysanthemums against the windows, thundering in a way that would punctuate the exact creak of the boards. Even today I am still conscious of the way my steps went nowhere. The dog did not bother to lift her head. The conspicuous absence of curtains, which was all my fault, like the way the lawn unfolded into ruin. In bed, the executioner is unlike any other man. I mean, it's not about power. The slip of paper I never put into my pocket saying *This is the last time I will ever*. I framed the entire scene in the doorway. After that, every stray basil leaf was a wonder.

MY GOODNESS

Bombs filled with thread. Glasses
wrapped in a cotton batting
virus. I read an eighteen-page letter

though only the parts about me,
or the lake, disregarding
all references to the legal system

or climate change, pieces of fabric
I once ripped off my skirt
when it got stuck in a train door

and maybe that was your fault,
in retrospect. We had so
much leisure, where did we get

away with it? Building a Bunsen
burner from scratch.
Taking up unnecessary petitions,

blah blah Saul Bellow, red beans
soaked not long enough,
one disastrous wedding, aluminum

scraps, people thinking we lived
in your car (we did,
sometimes), a friend with glorious

carpet. In the abandoned bread
factory you spoke of my
goodness. How some day old men

would want to bottle it. Other old
men would drown. You
said that it wasn't goodness at all

but now I think it was a mistake.
I should have left
myself in a cabinet by the door.

A COIN-OPERATED PARAMOUR AND A HALF

It was the first ever lung transplant
completed on a train, with nothing but thread
and good wishes. Nobody even looked

twice. I was that efficient. In the drug store
parking lot a man pounded on my car window
until it broke. I did not know him, or

maybe I did. He wanted directions
to the historic district. He wanted fingerless
mittens off what once passed for a sales rack,

or a series of digits to try in the payphone.
Back then you could lose a lung. Really.
That's why all the payphones were clustered

like nuns walking past a penitentiary.
You said it was a bad condition, elements
unfavorable for anything but watching sparks

that weren't even sparks. The post office
was an abandoned post office, even though
my father once walked me through

all the stones of the lobby. You were busy
counterfeiting your lungs, worshipping your
nothings. They weren't even sweet.

You said you would sleep out there
in the gazebo, on a red line train, curled up
like a lung next to its double, only the double

had been signed away to a donor. I didn't cost
you very much. A couple of quarters.
Enough thread to wrap around your finger.

INSIDE EVERY VENDING MACHINE IT'S 1979

There's no such thing as nostalgia
for artificial wood grain, especially when the color
mimics a wet pig yard in April. Nevertheless

we're trapped in an elevator, and the rug
is missing, and the walls are meant to imitate
the basements we all had and loved.

Some jackass shoved a vending machine
in here: a coin-operated elevator, with more
seductive ways of removing passengers.

Nothing left for sale but algae-green mints.
If only it had been the soda machine
that dropped its solitary paper cup, shuddered

its ounces with everyone as witness.
It's one box of wood grain inside another, and I
almost want to look down my shirt to verify

that it hasn't gotten to me. I'm not stocked
with anybody's marzipan octopus. Everything
is looking for a way out, or a way back in.

ACKNOWLEDGMENTS

Grateful acknowledgment is made to the editors of the following publications, where the poems below appeared, sometimes in slightly different versions.

The Account: A Tiny Poison Eye
Anti-: Some Dead Ingenuity, A Coin-Operated Railroad
Atticus Review: Revitalization Yields Questionable Results, Business Poem
Blackbird: A Coin-Operated Paramour and a Half, Coin-Operated Rattle without a Snake, Some Dead Magic
Crab Orchard Review: Pick-Your-Own
Devil's Lake: Some Discipline
diode: A Coin-Operated Gentrification Zone of the Heart, A Coin-Operated Apple Pie, A Coin-Operated Neighbor to the North, We Invent the Opposite of Vegas, Then Take it All Back
Escape into Life: A Coin-Operated Pickax, A Coin-Operated *How Do You Like Me Now*, A Coin-Operated Diary
Forklift, Ohio: My Goodness
Gulf Coast: Fight or Flight
The Jet Fuel Review: Elegy with Flickering Lights
Midwestern Gothic: Occupation: Hazard, The Fate of the Old Mill is Still Undecided
The National Poetry Review: In Which We Sense that We are Not Alone, A Coin-Operated Button-Down Collar
The Nepotist: Birth of a Vessel
Ninth Letter: Jewelry is for the Weak
Phoenix in the Jacuzzi Journal: Fortunes and Misfortunes
Redivider: A Coin-Operated Arboretum, Inside Every Vending Machine it's 1979

Revolution House: Burying the Apron
Slant (and Best of the Net): Miniatures
Sentence: A Journal of Prose Poetics: The Summer of Electronic Monitoring
South Dakota Review: An Elm Tree Will Never Be the One You Love, Coin-Operated Engine Finds its Steam
TAB: Version of Myself in the Ruins
Toad the Journal: Have Mercy on Me, A Sunny Place with Adequate Water, Inert, or Something Close
Thrush Poetry Journal: Parlor Games are for the Weak

The Academy of American Poets published, "In the Back Seat of History" as part of its Poem-A-Day on 7/11/13.

Many thanks to the friends and colleagues who believed in me and supported this project in one way or another: Julie Brooks Barbour, Heather Braun, Thomas Dukes, John Gallaher, David Giffels, Brian Harrell, Steve Kistulentz, Thea Ledendecker, Erika Meitner, Amy Peck, Bob Pope, Nate Pritts, Lee Ann Roripaugh, Jessica Schantz, Austin Seip, Carmen Giménez Smith, Amy Bracken Sparks, Bill Thelin, Heidi Thoenen, Greg Thompson, Elizabeth Tussey, Helen Vitoria, and Eric Wasserman. Special thanks, always, to Jay Robinson. Much gratitude to Black Lawrence Press, Diane Goettel, designer (and dear friend) Amy Freels, and cover artist Mark Brabant. Much love and gratitude to my parents, Patsy and Scott Biddinger, and to Eric, Gabi, and Ray.

A Sunny Place with Adequate Water is dedicated in memory of Melodee Berquist (1974–2010).

Mary Biddinger is the author of the poetry collections *Prairie Fever* (Steel Toe Books, 2007), *Saint Monica* (Black Lawrence Press, 2011), and *O Holy Insurgency* (Black Lawrence Press, 2013). She is also co-editor of *The Monkey and the Wrench: Essays into Contemporary Poetics* (U Akron Press, 2011). She teaches literature and poetry writing at The University of Akron, where she edits *Barn Owl Review*, the Akron Series in Poetry, and the Akron Series in Contemporary Poetics.